FISH

FISH

PERFECTLY PREPARED TO ENJOY EVERY DAY

This edition published in 2012
LOVE FOOD is an imprint of Parragon Books Ltd

Parragon
Chartist House
15–17 Trim Street
Bath BA1 1HE, UK

www.parragon.com/lovefood

ISBN: 978-1-78186-724-2

Printed in China

Concept: Patrik Jaros & Günter Beer
Recipes and food styling: Patrik Jaros www.foodlook.com
Text: Günter Beer, Gerhard von Richthofen, Patrik Jaros, Jörg Zipprick
Photography: Günter Beer www.beerfoto.com
Photographer's assistants: Sigurd Buchberger, Aranxa Alvarez
Cook's assistants: Magnus Thelen, Johannes von Bemberg
Designed by Estudio Merino www.estudiomerino.com
Produced by Buenavista Studio s.l. www.buenavistastudio.com
The visual index is a registered design of Buenavista Studio s.l. (European Trademark Office
number 000252796-001)
Project managment: trans texas publishing, Cologne
Typesetting: Nazire Ergün, Cologne

Notes for the Reader
This book uses standard kitchen measuring spoons and cups. All spoon and cup measurements are
level unless otherwise indicated. Unless otherwise stated, milk is assumed to be whole, butter is
assumed to be salted, eggs are large, individual vegetables are medium, and pepper is freshly ground
black pepper. Unless otherwise stated, all root vegetables should be washed and peeled before using.

Garnishes and serving suggestions are all optional and not necessarily included in the recipe
ingredients or method. The times given are only an approximate guide. Preparation times differ
according to the techniques used by different people and the cooking times may also vary from
those given. Optional ingredients, variations, or serving suggestions have not been included in
the calculations.

Recipes using raw or very lightly cooked eggs should be avoided by infants, the elderly, pregnant
women, and people with weakened immune systems. Pregnant and breast-feeding women are advised
to avoid eating peanuts and peanut products. People with nut allergies should be aware that some
of the prepared ingredients used in the recipes in this book may contain nuts. Always check the
packaging before use.

The publisher would advise using fish and seafood from sustainable sources.

Picture acknowledgments
All photos by Günter Beer, Barcelona

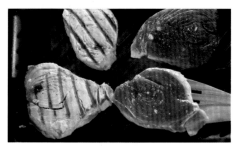

Contents

Introduction

Fresh fish and seafood are tasty, versatile, and exceptionally healthy foods. For example, fish is rich in valuable protein, vitamins, minerals, and unsaturated fatty acids. Oily fish, such as salmon, mackerel, and tuna also contain so-called omega-3 fatty acids. These have a particularly positive effect on our cardiovascular system, but they are not produced by our own bodies, which is why health experts recommend that we eat freshly prepared fish at least once a week.

Many types of fish and seafood are very low in fat and are, therefore, an essential part of a healthy diet, especially a weight-watching diet. Moreover, most varieties of white fish, shellfish, or octopus are easily digestible. Fish and seafood are valued not least of all for their exquisitely fine flavor and, for good reason, are regarded as the delicacies of the sea. Not surprisingly, they are used to prepare wonderfully tasty dishes all around the world.

This is also reflected in the choice of recipes featured in this book. From Trout Meunière and the Japanese-inspired Sesame-Coated Tuna Sticks, to the Mediterranean Monkfish Medallions on a Tomato & Caper Ragout, there is something for every taste and occasion.

Fish and seafood can be served either as an appetizer, in the form of soup, antipasti or salad, or as a main dish, for example as a whole fish, filleted with side dishes, or as a one-dish meal.

Buying and storing fish
Fish and seafood are highly perishable, so they should be purchased freshly caught and eaten at the latest two to three days after being caught. Fish should always have a slightly salty aroma and never smell bad or of ammonia. A shiny, firm body with intact skin and scales, bright eyes, and light pink to reddish gills are also signs of freshness. The shells of fresh shellfish should never be damaged. They should also smell fresh and of the sea and on no account have an unpleasant odor. Fresh mussels close when touched. If they do not close, are damaged, or fail to open after cooking, they should be discarded at once.

Nowadays, many types of fish and seafood are frozen on board fishing vessels before being transported elsewhere. If you're not lucky enough to have a good fish dealer nearby, frozen products are your best choice. Frozen fish can be kept in the freezer for between two and five months, depending on the freezer type. To thaw, place the fish on a plate, cover, and let stand in the

refrigerator for several hours, preferably overnight. Place seafood in a bowl, cover with a cloth, and let thaw in the refrigerator overnight. Do not refreeze once thawed. Fish and seafood should be transported in a cool bag after purchasing and, if possible, prepared on the day of purchase or within 24 hours.

Preparation
There are numerous types of fish and seafood available, just as there are numerous ways to prepare them. Smaller varieties of fish, pieces of fish, shrimp, and octopus rings are ideal for deep-frying. First, coat in bread crumbs to prevent the fish from becoming too dry. This keeps the flesh succulent while the coating turns crisp and golden brown. Heat the oil to 350–375°F, so that the coating does not soak up too much fat and stays crisp. If you are deep-frying large quantities, do this in batches to prevent the temperature in the deep-fryer from dropping and the fish from becoming soggy and unappetizing.

Whole fish, fillets, and shellfish can also be shallow-fried in a skillet. Before cooking, coat the fish in flour. Again, make sure the fat in the skillet is hot enough before adding the fish, and avoid overcrowding. Sauté fillets on the skin side first, and then briefly on the flesh side. This guarantees that the skin will become crispy and the flesh will remain succulent and full of flavor.

Fish and shellfish can also be cooked in liquid. However, fish should not be left to simmer for too long because it falls apart easily, while shellfish tends to become tough if overcooked. A wonderful way to cook whole fish and shellfish in liquid is to poach them in stock, wine, or water. Remember to keep the liquid below boiling point to prevent the fish from falling apart while cooking.

Whole and stuffed fish, fish fillets and steaks, as well as shellfish, can also be baked in the oven. A little liquid, oil or melted butter is poured over the fish to prevent it from drying out. The fish can also be covered with a lid, foil, or a salty crust. A particularly low-fat method of preparing fish is to steam it. The fish is placed on a steamer pan over a saucepan of boiling liquid and is cooked gently. This method of cooking also preserves valuable nutrients.

In the summer, of course, fish and shellfish can also be grilled over a barbecue. For a tasty result, simply brush the fish with oil mixed with lemon juice and herbs. This is a quick and easy way to prepare delicious fish and shrimp brochettes as well as whole fish. However, whole fish or pieces of fish should not be more than 2 inches thick, otherwise they will not cook through properly.

With fresh fish and shellfish, you can treat yourself, your family, and friends to a wide variety of healthy and highly nutritious dishes that are simple to prepare and delicious to eat.

How to use this book

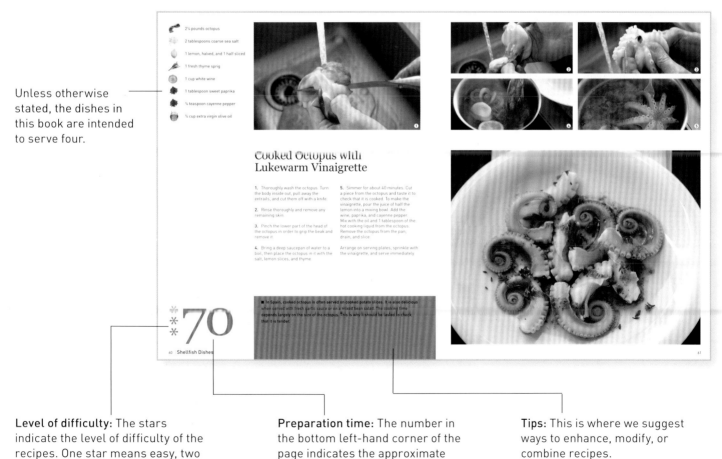

Unless otherwise stated, the dishes in this book are intended to serve four.

Level of difficulty: The stars indicate the level of difficulty of the recipes. One star means easy, two intermediate, three difficult.

Preparation time: The number in the bottom left-hand corner of the page indicates the approximate preparation time in minutes.

Tips: This is where we suggest ways to enhance, modify, or combine recipes.

Cleaning & Descaling Fish

Ask your fish dealer to gut the fish and cut the gills before you take it home.

Cut off the pelvic fins with scissors.

Use sharp kitchen scissors to cut off the pectoral fins.

Trim the tail fin by half, otherwise it could burn during pan-frying.

Use a small kitchen knife to scale the fish.

Rinse well under running water and wash off any blood and pieces of skin.

If you descale the fish under running water, the scales will be rinsed off by the water instead of flying all over the kitchen.

Remove the excess water by hand.

Place the fish on paper towels and make a small slit in the skin from the head to the tail fin. It is easier to get the knife under the flesh to fillet the fish this way, and it prevents the skin from tearing irregularly during cooking.

How to Fillet Fish

Place the fish on a cutting board to fillet it.

Using a knife, cut at an angle from the head to the backbone.

Turn the blade toward the tail fin and make a small cut.

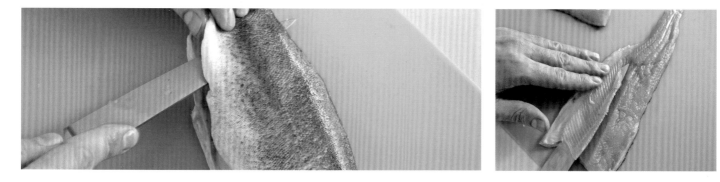

Push the knife along the backbone and cut off the fillet. Make sure that the top fillet is always stretched, which will make the job easier. Remove the fillet with the knife all the way to the tail fin. Turn the fish over and remove the bottom fillet.

Remove the rib cage without cutting away too much flesh and put the trimmings aside.

Separate the fillet from the skin. Hold the skin with one hand and, with your other hand, remove the fillet using the knife.

Remove the small bones with fish pliers.

The leftovers from filleting can be used to prepare fish stock later. Stock from freshwater fish is sometimes cloudy and does not have the distinctive taste of saltwater fish stock.

1 bunch fresh dill

3 cucumbers

1¾ pounds salmon fillet, skinned

½ horseradish root, grated

1 lemon

4 tablespoons butter

salt and white pepper, to taste

pinch of sugar

1 cup fish stock

½ cup heavy cream

½ cup crème fraîche or sour cream

2 tablespoons heavy cream, whipped

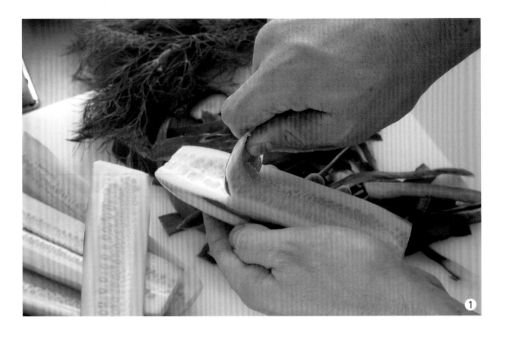

Salmon Fillets with Horseradish Butter & Dill Pickles

1. Wash the dill and set it aside. Peel the cucumbers, halve them lengthwise, and remove the seeds with a small spoon. Cut the cucumbers diagonally into ½-inch thick slices.

2. Skin and clean the salmon, remove any bones with fish pliers, and cut the fillet into four equal portions. Marinate the fillets with the horseradish and the juice of half the lemon. Cut the other half lemon into thin slices.

3. Melt 2 tablespoons of the butter in a wide saucepan over medium heat and add the cucumber slices. Season with salt and pepper, add the sugar, and sauté briefly. Add the stock and simmer for about 5 minutes, until it is reduced by half.

4. Add the cream and the crème fraîche and simmer for 1 minute. Finely chop the dill, mix with the whipped cream, then add the mixture to the cucumbers.

5. In the meantime, melt the remaining butter in a nonstick skillet. Season the marinated salmon fillets and place in the skillet. Slowly sauté on both sides for about 3 minutes, while pouring the butter from the skillet over them.

Arrange the cooked cucumbers on plates, place a piece of salmon on each plate, and garnish with a slice of lemon.

■ You can prepare a horseradish crust for the salmon pieces by beating 4 tablespoons of butter until creamy, then adding 2 egg yolks, 2 tablespoons of grated horseradish, and 2 cups of fresh white bread crumbs. Mix the ingredients and season with salt and pepper. Pour the mixture over the raw salmon pieces and place them in a buttered soufflé dish. Pour ½ cup of white wine over the fish and bake at 350°F for 15 minutes, until golden brown.

1¼ sticks butter, plus extra for greasing

 large bunch fresh dill

bunch fresh parsley

1 egg yolk

salt and white pepper, to taste

2 tablespoons bread crumbs

4 salmon fillets, about 7 ounces each, skinned

½ cup dry white wine

1 lemon

Slow Roasted Salmon

1. Preheat the oven to 225°F. Grease a soufflé dish. Put the butter in a small mixing bowl and beat until creamy. Finely chop the dill and the parsley. Mix the egg yolk with the butter and the herbs. Season with salt and pepper. Carefully mix in the bread crumbs and adjust the seasoning, if necessary.

2. Season the salmon fillets with salt, place them in the prepared dish, and brush on the herb butter.

3. Pour the wine over the fish. Slice the lemon and add one slice to each fillet.

4. Cook the salmon in the preheated oven for 30–35 minutes.

Remove from the oven and serve with white bread.

■ Vary this salmon dish by chopping the herbs together with 1 tablespoon of ginger and 1 bunch of fresh cilantro and adding the butter. Then continue as described above.

 4 trout, about 9 ounces each

salt, to taste

flour, for dusting

¼ cup vegetable oil

5 tablespoons butter

bunch fresh parsley, finely chopped

juice of 1 lemon

Trout Meunière

1. Gut the trout, if necessary, and descale, clean, and drain them. Season the fish inside and outside with salt and dust them lightly with flour.

2. Heat the oil in a large skillet, place the trout in the skillet, and cook for about 5–7 minutes on each side. When each trout is golden brown on both sides, remove the oil from the skillet, using a tablespoon.

3. Add the butter to the skillet, sprinkle the parsley over the fish, and sauté. Add the lemon juice to the skillet, then transfer the fish to a serving dish and serve immediately.

* * * **35**

4 trout, about 9 ounces each

salt, to taste

flour, for dusting

¼ cup vegetable oil

5 tablespoons butter

½ cup slivered almonds

juice of 1 lemon

Trout Amandine

1. Gut the trout, if necessary, and descale, clean, and drain them. Season the fish inside and outside with salt and dust them lightly with flour.

2. Heat the oil in a large skillet, place the trout in the skillet, and cook for about 5–7 minutes on each side. When each trout is golden brown on both sides, re-move the oil from the skillet, using a tablespoon.

3. Add the butter and the slivered almonds to the skillet and sauté. The almonds should be light golden brown. Add the lemon juice, transfer the fish to a serving dish, and serve immediately.

* * * **35**

1 cup red wine

½ cup port

pinch of sugar

⅔ cup heavy cream

salt and pepper, to taste

1 stick butter

1 pound fresh spinach

freshly grated nutmeg

4 John Dory, flounder, or tilapia fillets, about 5–5¾ ounces each

juice of ½ lemon

2 tablespoons vegetable oil

8 fresh lemon thyme sprigs

①

Poached John Dory in a Red Wine & Butter Sauce

1. Combine the wine and port with the sugar in a saucepan, bring to a boil, and cook until the liquid has reduced to about one sixth of its volume.

2. Add ¼ cup of the cream and bring to a boil. Season with salt and pepper.

3. Cut 4 tablespoons of the butter into thin slices and place in the wine reduction to bind it. Set the sauce aside.

4. Melt 2 tablespoons of the butter in a saucepan until it foams, add the spinach leaves, and let them sauté. Season with salt, pepper, and nutmeg. Add the remaining cream and slowly simmer for an additional 2 minutes.

5. Using a kitchen knife, trim the fish fillets, sprinkle the lemon juice over them, and season with salt on both sides. Heat the remaining butter and the oil in a nonstick saucepan. Place the fillets in the pan and top each with a sprig of lemon thyme. Pour some butter over the fish occasionally and slowly sauté for about 3 minutes on each side, until they are lightly browned.

Arrange some spinach in the middle of four plates and carefully pour the reserved sauce around. Place a fish fillet on top and garnish with lemon thyme.

■ A good-quality red wine is an absolute must for a flavorful red wine and butter sauce. Leeks or Swiss chard can be substituted for the spinach.

✳
✳ 40
✳

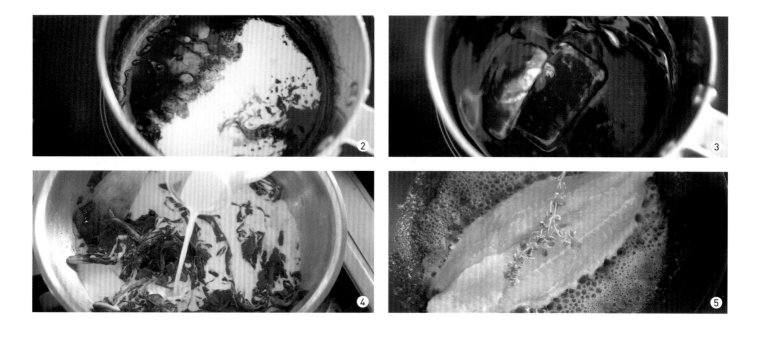

4 catfish fillets, about 5–5¾ ounces each, skinned

1 leek

1 large carrot

¼ head celeriac

3 cups water

salt, to taste

3 tablespoons white wine vinegar or cider vinegar

1 onion

1 bay leaf

1 clove

⅔ cup fish stock

3 tablespoons cold butter

small bunch fresh chives, snipped

½ horseradish root, grated

Catfish in Root Vegetable Stock

1. Using a knife, trim the catfish fillets and cut them in half. Slice the leeks, carrots, and celeriac into long thin strips. Put the water into a large saucepan with 2 tablespoons of salt and the vinegar. Stud the onion with the bay leaf and clove, and place it in the pan. Bring to a boil and simmer for 5 minutes. Place the catfish in this stock, remove from the heat, and let stand for 8–10 minutes. Meanwhile, bring a saucepan of lightly salted water to a boil, add the vegetable strips, bring back to a boil, and cook for about 1 minute, then refresh the vegetables in cold water.

2. Combine the fish stock with 1 cup of the cooking stock, strain into a saucepan, bring to a boil, and cook for 5 minutes to reduce the liquid. Add the butter, using a wire whisk to blend the stock more easily. Finely chop the chives.

3. Place the vegetable strips and the catfish fillets in the stock and bring to a boil. Serve in soup bowls, garnished with the chives and horseradish.

■ Cod fillets can be prepared in the same way. However, increase the cooking time to 8 minutes and add 1 teaspoon of mustard to the stock for extra flavor.

45

1

2

4 catfish fillets, about
5–5¾ ounces each, skinned

juice of 1 lemon

salt and white pepper, to taste

sweet paprika, to taste

1 tablespoon extra virgin olive oil

3 cups Paprika
Cream Sauce (see below)

2 tablespoons heavy cream,
whipped

Catfish in Paprika Sauce

1. Using a knife, trim the skinned catfish fillets and cut into ¾-inch strips. Place in a bowl and sprinkle with the lemon juice. Season with salt, pepper, and paprika. Add the oil and mix. Marinate for about 10 minutes.

2. Pour the paprika cream sauce into a saucepan and bring to a boil. Place the marinated strips of catfish in the sauce and reheat slowly for about 3 minutes. Do not let boil, because this will make the fish tough.

Mix in the whipped cream and arrange on plates to serve.

■ To make the Paprika Cream Sauce, dice 4 red bell peppers. Thinly slice 1 onion and 2 garlic cloves. Heat ¼ cup of extra virgin olive oil in a saucepan, add the onion and garlic, and sauté until translucent. Add 1 thyme sprig, 2 bay leaves, and the red bell pepper, then add 1 tablespoon of sugar and season with salt and pepper. Pour in ½ cup of white wine and about 2½ cups of chicken stock and simmer for about 15 minutes. Remove the herbs and mix the sauce with an immersion blender. Pass the mixture through a fine strainer, pressing the vegetables through so that the sauce is rich and thick.

20

2 carp fillets

1 pinch salt
1 pinch black pepper

2 lemons

2 eggs

¾ cup flour

5 cups dried bread crumbs

¼ cup oil

4 tablespoons butter

Carp Fried in Batter

1. Descale the carp fillets and clean with paper towels. Hold the fish with one hand while carefully removing the bones with fish pliers.

2. Cut the fillets into 1¼-inch-wide strips and feel with your fingers for any remaining bones. If necessary, use the fish pliers again.

3. Season the carp strips with the salt and pepper. Halve one of the lemons and rub the fish on both sides with a lemon half. Slice the other lemon into small wedges and reserve as a garnish.

4. Beat the eggs in a shallow dish. Spread the flour on the bottom of a separate shallow dish and put the bread crumbs in a dish or plate. Dip the carp strips into the flour to coat both sides, then dip them in the egg mixture. Dip in the bread crumbs to coat and gently press the bread crumbs in place.

5. Melt the oil and butter in a large skillet, add the carp pieces, and cook on both sides for about 8 minutes, until golden brown.

Place on paper towels to drain, then serve with the lemon wedges and a potato and vegetable salad.

* * * 90

■ Carp is predominantly used in gefilte fish, or stuffed fish, a traditional Jewish dish. If you use a large carp, remove the skin with a long, sharp kitchen knife to prevent the dish from becoming too fatty. It is best to use a carp approximately 2¼–3¼ pounds in weight.

1 eggplant

salt, to taste

⅓ cup extra virgin olive oil

1 teaspoon tandoori powder

2 red onions, finely chopped

3 tomatoes, peeled and diced

10 fresh basil leaves, chopped

1-inch piece fresh ginger, peeled and finely grated

4 limes

pepper, to taste

1¾-pound tuna fillet

Tuna Steaks

1. Cut the eggplant into ½-inch-thick slices and season with salt. Add 2 tablespoons of the oil to a skillet, add the eggplant slices, and sauté on both sides. Mix the tandoori powder with 2 tablespoons of the oil in a small bowl and lightly season with salt.

2. Combine the onions, tomatoes, basil, and ginger in a bowl with the juice of two of the limes. Season with salt and pepper.

3. Cut the tuna fillet into 1¼-inch-thick steaks, spread the remaining oil over them and season with salt. Cut the two remaining limes in half.

4. Heat a nonstick ridged grill pan, add the tuna steaks, and cook for 2 minutes on each side.

Divide the tomato-onion mixture among four serving plates and arrange the sautéed eggplant slices and tuna steaks over it. Garnish with the tandoori oil and lime halves, and serve.

■ Tuna remains fresh for longer if sliced shortly before cooking.

*
*
* 40

1¼-pound tuna fillet

1 teaspoon roasted sesame oil

½ cup black sesame seeds

½ cup white sesame seeds

1 lemon, sliced

chili oil, for sprinkling

soy sauce, to serve

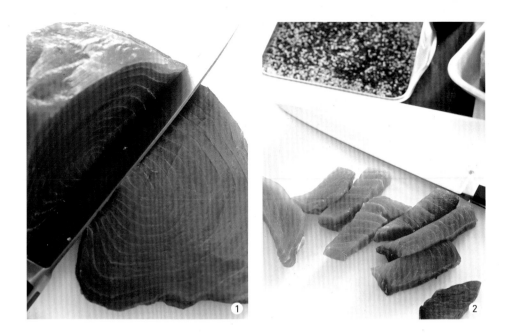

Sesame-Coated Tuna Sticks

1. Pat dry the tuna fillet, remove any tendons, and cut into ½-inch-thick slices.

2. Cut the slices into ¾-inch-thick strips.

3. Sprinkle the roasted sesame oil over the strips and turn them so that they are evenly coated.

4. Place the tuna pieces in a baking pan with the mixed black and white sesame seeds, turning the fish over to coat them on all sides with the seeds.

5. Put the fish in a nonstick skillet and cook without oil for about 1 minute. The tuna should be slightly raw on the inside. If you prefer it well done, double the cooking time.

Arrange the tuna sticks on a serving plate, add the lemon slices, sprinkle a little chili oil over them, and serve with soy sauce.

✳
✳ 15
✳

■ The sesame seeds can be mixed with chopped fennel seeds, coriander seeds, or a few Sichuan peppercorns. This will give the tuna sticks more zest and aroma.

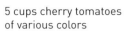

- 2 shallots
- 5 cups cherry tomatoes of various colors
- 1 tablespoon capers
- 1 garlic clove
- small bunch fresh basil
- 3¼-pound monkfish tail
- 1 fresh thyme sprig
- 2 tablespoons butter
- 2 tablespoons extra virgin olive oil
- salt, to taste
- sugar, to taste
- pepper, to taste
- 2 cups fish stock
- 2 tablespoons sunflower oil
- sea salt, to taste
- 1 tablespoon coarse mustard

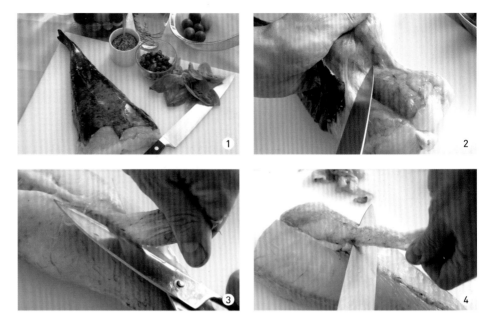

Monkfish Medallions on a Tomato & Caper Ragout

1. Dice the shallots. Peel the tomatoes. Chop the capers. Peel and dice the garlic. Chop the basil into fine strips.

2. Prepare the monkfish. First, remove the outer skin by holding it taut with your left hand and cutting it with the tip of a sharp knife. Pull off the last 4 inches of the skin with your fingers.

3. Use scissors to cut off the dorsal and ventral fins.

4. Carefully remove the top layer of the skin with a sharp knife. Cut the fish into 1¼-inch-thick slices.

5. Pluck the thyme leaves off the stems and sprinkle them over the monkfish.

6. Melt one third of the butter with the olive oil in a saucepan over medium heat, add the garlic and shallots, and brown. Add the tomatoes and season with salt, sugar and pepper. Reduce the temperature to low. Pour in the fish stock and add sea salt, stir in the mustard, and simmer for 7 minutes.

■ The range of tomatoes adds a variety of both color and flavor to the ragout.

*** 50

7. Pour the sunflower oil into a skillet, add the monkfish, and sauté on each side for 2–3 minutes over medium–high heat. Season with sea salt.

8. Add the capers, basil, and the remaining butter to the tomatoes and lightly toss in the pan.

Arrange the finished tomato ragout on serving plates, place the monkfish on top, and serve immediately.

3 eggs

2⅓ cups all-purpose flour

1 teaspoon baking powder

salt, to taste

1½ cups beer

1¼-pound salmon fillet

white pepper, to taste

juice of ½ lemon

9 cups vegetable oil, for frying

Salmon in Beer Batter

1. Separate the eggs and refrigerate the egg whites. Pour the flour into a mixing bowl. Add the egg yolks, baking powder, and a pinch of salt.

2. Gradually add the beer, beating until the batter is smooth.

3. Beat the egg whites with a pinch of salt until holding soft peaks, and carefully fold into the batter.

4. Cut the salmon fillets into bite-size pieces, season with salt and pepper, sprinkle some lemon juice over them, and carefully dip them in the batter.

5. Meanwhile heat the oil in a large saucepan to 325°F. Add the salmon and cook for about 5 minutes, then turn. Drain on paper towels.

Serve immediately, with lemon wedges for squeezing over the fish.

■ To prevent the fat from splattering, it is best to use a deep saucepan.

 ½ leek

5 button mushrooms

3 tablespoons butter

4 red snapper fillets, about 6 ounces each

salt, to taste

white pepper, to taste

3 tablespoons vermouth

⅔ cup white wine

1 tablespoon fresh basil leaves

Sautéed Red Snapper Fillets in White Wine and Mushrooms

1. Cut the leek in half lengthwise and slice into thin strips. Thinly slice the mushrooms. Heat 2 tablespoons of the butter in a skillet until foaming, then add the leek and mushrooms and season with a little salt.

2. Pat the fish fillets dry with paper towels and season with salt and pepper. Put the fish on top of the vegetables in the skillet.

3. Add the vermouth and wine and reduce the heat.

4. Sprinkle with the basil leaves, cover, and steam for about 5 minutes, then add the remaining cold butter.

Serve immediately with potatoes or rice.

■ Try this dish with sea bass or halibut fillets instead of the red snapper and serve with a simple butter sauce.

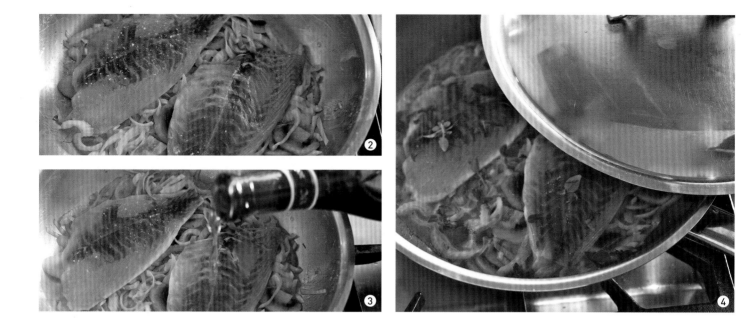

8 cups coarse sea salt
(about 4½ pounds)

2¼-pound red snapper, unscaled

1 fennel slice

1 lime slice

10 white peppercorns

1 fresh rosemary sprig

fennel greens

White Fish Baked in a Salt Crust

1. Preheat the oven to 450°F. Moisten the salt with a little water and mix.

2. Fill the prepared fish with the fennel slice, lime slice, peppercorns, rosemary, and fennel greens. Then close up the fish so that no salt crust can get inside it.

3. Place some parchment paper on a baking sheet and add a ½-inch layer of the damp salt. Place the fish on top and cover with the remaining salt.

4. Pat down the salt around the fish to form the shape of a fish.

5. Put the fish in the preheated oven and cook for about 35 minutes. Break open the salt crust and remove the fish.

6. Cut the skin along the backbone, and then use a spoon and a knife to skin the fish.

7. Carefully remove the fillets, making sure that the fish does not come into contact with the salt crust.

Place the fillets on a serving plate and reassemble them. Serve with fresh bread or rosemary potatoes.

50

■ Prepare a light vinaigrette using diced tomatoes, olive oil, lemon juice, fennel greens, and salt and pepper, and drizzle it over the fish fillets.

2 sole

salt, to taste

8 ounces white fish fillet, such as cod

¼ cup heavy cream

cayenne pepper, to taste

bunch fresh flat-leaf parsley, plus extra sprigs to garnish

10 fresh basil leaves

2 fresh tarragon sprigs

small bunch fresh chives

3 russet potatoes

⅔ cup Clarified Butter (see below)

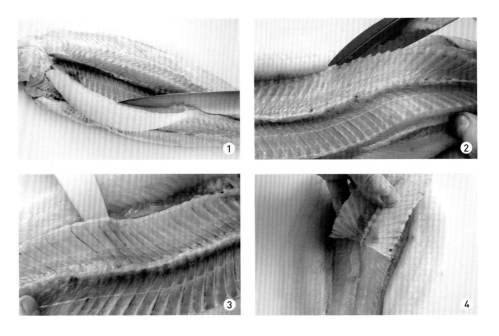

Stuffed Sole Garnished with Potato Scales

1. Use a sharp flexible knife to cut the prepared sole along their backbones. Slowly loosen the fillets until the center bone is clearly visible but the fillets are still attached to the sole.

2. Using kitchen scissors, separate the outside of the center bone, starting from the tail.

3. Using the knife, cut along the center bone to loosen it.

4. Bend the center bone, which is now only attached at one point, from the tail end up and gradually pull out. Season the sole on the inside and outside with salt.

5. Cut the white fish fillet into cubes and place in the freezer for 5 minutes. Place the chilled fish cubes in a food processor, add the cream, and mix until smooth. Season with salt and cayenne pepper. Finely chop the parsley, basil, tarragon, and chives and add to the mixture. Spread the filling on the open sole.

6. Close the fillets. This brings the sole back to their original shape.

7. Peel the potatoes and slice paper-thin. Place 3 slices on top of each other and cut out ¾-inch circles.

■ To make Clarified Butter, put the butter in a saucepan over low heat and gently melt. Skim off any froth that appears on the surface—this will reveal a clear yellow layer on top of a milky layer. Pour the clear fat into a bowl or pitcher, discarding the milky residue. Clarified butter will keep in the refrigerator for several weeks and can be frozen for longer.

8. Place the potato slices in a scale-like pattern on the sole, generously brush on the clarified butter, then season with salt.

9. Place the sole in the freezer for 3 minutes, so the butter solidifies and the sole can be placed in a skillet without the potato scales moving around. Put the fish, scales down, in a nonstick skillet over medium heat and slowly sauté. Tilt the skillet occasionally and use a spoon to pour the liquid in the skillet over the sole. Carefully turn after 5 minutes and sauté for an additional 5 minutes.

Serve immediately, garnished with lemon wedges and sprigs of flat-leaf parsley.

small bunch fresh sage

bunch fresh parsley

1 pound small new potatoes

4 sole

salt, to taste

1 lemon

¼ cup all-purpose flour

¼ cup sunflower oil

1 stick butter

Sole in Sage Butter

1. Take the sage leaves off their stems. Chop the parsley. Peel the potatoes. Bring a saucepan of lightly salted water to a boil, add the potatoes, bring back to a boil, and cook until tender. Slit the fish on both sides along the backbone. This makes it easier to remove the bones later. Season with salt and sprinkle some lemon juice over the fish. Dust with flour, removing any excess. Heat a large skillet over medium heat, add the oil, then add the fish and cook on the white-skinned side for 5 minutes, until golden brown. Turn and cook for an additional 5 minutes, then spoon out the oil, add 5 tablespoons of butter, and let it foam.

2. Recook the fish in the butter, basting occasionally. Drain the potatoes. Add the remaining butter and the parsley to the potatoes and season with salt.

3. Add the sage leaves to the skillet and continue to pour butter over the sole until the sage leaves are crisp. Arrange the potatoes on serving plates. Place the whole fish on each plate and pour the sage butter over them.

Serve immediately with the parsley potatoes on the side.

60

■ The bones of a fried sole can be carefully removed with a spoon. Serve sole with fresh spinach or white wine sauce.

2 turbot, about 1¾ pounds each

salt and white pepper, to taste

¼ cup all-purpose flour

¼ cup vegetable oil

4 tablespoons butter

½ bunch fresh parsley

juice of 1 lemon

❶

Turbot Fillet Fried on the Bone

1. Fillet the turbot along the backbone. Season both sides of the turbot fillets with salt and pepper and lightly dust with flour. Remove any excess flour. Heat the oil in a large skillet. Add the turbot and cook for 5 minutes on the dark-skinned side, continually basting the fish with oil from the skillet. Turn and cook on the other side for an additional 5 minutes.

2. Remove the oil from the skillet, add the butter, and slowly sauté the turbot over low heat for 2 minutes, making sure that the butter doesn't get too brown.

3. While the turbot is still in the skillet, remove the dark skin. It will be easy to remove from the cooked fish. Season with salt.

4. Chop the parsley and add to the skillet with the lemon juice. Slightly tilt the skillet and continue to baste butter from the skillet over the turbot.

Place the fish on serving plates, pour the parsley butter over the fish, and serve immediately.

■ As an alternative, you can prepare one 10-ounce turbot fillet per person. Tarragon, basil, and chives can be substituted for the parsley.

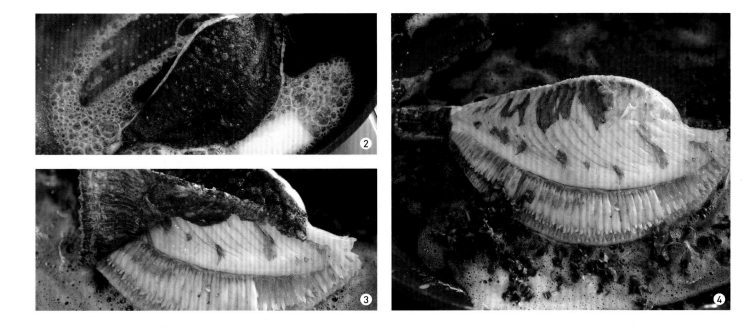

8 ounces sardines

2 tablespoons flour

9 cups vegetable oil, for frying

salt, to taste

lemon wedges, to serve

Fried Sardines

1. Clean the sardines under cold running water. Slowly break away the head towards the top, pulling out the innards at the same time.

2. Open the stomach with your thumb and wash it thoroughly. After removing the head you can loosen the backbone and remove it completely, if desired.

3. Place the sardines or sardine fillets in a strainer, pat dry, and sprinkle with the flour.

4. Hold the strainer over the sink and shake off any excess flour.

5. Put the oil into a wide saucepan and heat to 340°F. Add the sardines and cook for 2 minutes for whole sardines, or 1 minute for fillets. Remove from the oil and drain on paper towels. Season with salt.

Serve immediately with lemon wedges.

15

■ Italian-style sardines are marinated in balsamic vinegar and olive oil and served cold with white bread.

8 garlic cloves

small bunch fresh parsley

2 dried jalapeño chiles

2¼ pounds raw jumbo shrimp

⅔ cup extra virgin olive oil

coarse sea salt, to taste

a few drops of lemon juice

Garlic Shrimp

1. Peel the garlic and thinly slice. Chop the parsley. Lightly press down on the chiles. Peel the shrimp.

2. Heat the oil in a skillet over medium heat, add the chiles and garlic, and cook until lightly browned.

3. After about 1 minute, add the shrimp and sauté for an additional 2 minutes. Add the parsley and season with salt and a few drops of lemon juice.

Serve immediately with fresh white bread or cooked rice.

■ Mix some chopped cooked spaghetti and a few tomato cubes into the garlic shrimp. Add a few spoons of cooking water so that the oil binds better with the pasta.

1 small pineapple

1 pound cooked shrimp

1¼ cups Cocktail Sauce
(see below)

4 orange slices

4 celery leaves

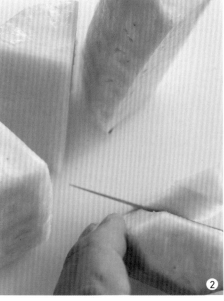

Shrimp Cocktail

1. Cut off the pineapple skin with a knife.

2. Cut the pineapple into quarters lengthwise and cut out the core and any remaining brown 'eyes'.

3. Cut the pineapple in ¼-inch cubes, about the size of the shrimp.

4. Place the shrimp and the pineapple in a bowl, add the cocktail sauce, and mix.

Serve in small bowls, garnished with orange slices and some celery leaves.

■ To make Cocktail Sauce, add 3 tablespoons of ketchup, 2 teaspoons of grated horseradish, 3 tablespoons of cognac, and the juice of ½ an orange to 1 cup of mayonnaise. Blend with a whisk until smooth. Add a pinch of salt, a pinch of cayenne pepper, and 3 drops of Worcestershire sauce.

8 scallops

 8 bacon strips

1 tablespoon vegetable oil

salt and pepper, to taste

½ cup coarse sea salt, to serve

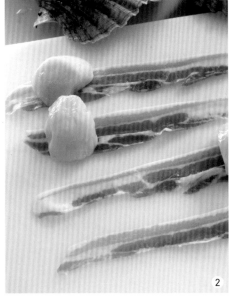

Fried Scallops Wrapped in Bacon

1. Remove the white flesh from the scallop shells. Clean the bottom shell, remove any remaining parts of the corals and reserve. Dry the shells and set aside until the dish is ready to serve.

2. Lay the bacon strips on a work surface. Place the white scallop flesh on one end and roll up in the bacon.

3. Heat a little of the vegetable oil in a skillet. Place the bacon-wrapped scallops in the skillet and season with pepper. Do not add salt, because the bacon provides plenty of flavor.

4. Pan-fry the scallops on both sides for about 1 minute, until the bacon is crisp.

5. Place the reserved corals in a separate skillet with the remaining oil and quickly cook on both sides. Season lightly with salt and pepper. Sprinkle the sea salt on small serving plates and arrange the shells firmly on it. Place the bacon-wrapped scallops in the shells.

Garnish with the sautéed corals and serve immediately.

■ This dish is served as an appetizer. However, the scallops can be cooked without the bacon and served with asparagus salad or in pumpkin soup.

2 cups fresh white bread crumbs

10 ounces crabmeat

small bunch fresh cilantro

2 tablespoons crème fraîche or sour cream

3 eggs

salt, to taste

pepper, to taste

2 tablespoons vegetable oil

Crispy Crab Cakes

1. Put the crabmeat into a mixing bowl and crush with a fork so it will be easier to mix with the other ingredients.

2. Finely chop the cilantro. Add the crème fraîche to the crabmeat. Separate 2 eggs and add the yolks to the crabmeat with the remaining whole egg. Season with salt and pepper and mix in the cilantro.

3. Add half the bread crumbs and mix. Cover and chill in the refrigerator for 15 minutes. The mixture is easier to work with when cold.

4. Using a tablespoon, take some of the mixture from the bowl and shape into cakes by hand. Dip the crab cakes into the remaining bread crumbs.

5. Heat the oil in a nonstick skillet. Add the crab cakes and cook on both sides for 2–3 minutes, until golden brown, turning them over carefully.

Arrange the crab cakes on plates and serve with a dip.

45

■ Dip recommendation: Pour 1 cup ketchup into a mixing bowl, add 1 teaspoon of finely grated fresh ginger, and mix in a few drops of Tabasco sauce. The cakes can also be prepared with chopped shrimp or with leftovers of other cooked shellfish instead of the crabmeat.

4½ pounds live crayfish

3 carrots

3 scallions

3 shallots

2 leeks

4 celery stalks

1 garlic clove

large bunch fresh dill

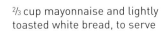

5 cloves

1 teaspoon black peppercorns

3 bay leaves

1 dried jalapeño chile

2 cups white wine

2 tablespoons coarse sea salt

⅔ cup mayonnaise and lightly toasted white bread, to serve

Crayfish in Dill Stock

1. First check that the crayfish are still moving; if not, discard them. Peel the carrots, scallions, and shallots. Cut the leeks in half. Cut the celery and the other vegetables into ¼-inch slices. Crush the garlic clove in its skin. Chop the dill, reserving a few sprigs to garnish.

2. Pour 20 cups (5 quarts) of water into a large stockpot with the cloves, peppercorns, bay leaves, chile, wine, and salt and bring to a boil. Add the vegetables and the dill and simmer for 3 minutes.

3. Place half of the crayfish in the simmering stock. Cover with a lid and immediately bring back to a boil. When the crayfish have turned red, remove them with a large skimming ladle. Add the remaining crayfish and cook.

Break away the tails and arrange the crayfish on a plate with some mayonnaise and the reserved dill sprigs. Serve with lightly toasted white bread.

40

■ Serve the crayfish in a large bowl placed in the center of the table, so that everyone can help themselves. Savor the crayfish during the summer months with a fresh white wine and some Cocktail Sauce (see page 44).

4 ears of corn

4 lobsters

coarse sea salt, to taste

cayenne pepper, to taste

1 stick butter

fine sea salt

Boiled Lobster with Corn Ears & Melted Butter

1. Remove the leaves and silks from the ears of corn, and cut off the stems. Add water to a saucepan large enough to hold all the corn cobs and bring to a boil. Do not add any salt to the water—it could make the corn tough.

2. Place the corn in the boiling water and simmer for 8 minutes.

3. Using a knife, remove the rubber bands from the lobster pincers. Fill a large stockpot with 20 cups (4 quarts) of water and bring to a boil. Season with coarse sea salt and cayenne pepper.

4. Put the lobster into the boiling water head-first and bring the water back to a boil. Reduce the heat and simmer for 10 minutes.

5. Melt the butter in a small saucepan. Arrange the lobster on four serving plates. Add one corn cob to each plate, drizzle with the melted butter, and sprinkle with some fine sea salt.

Serve immediately, with lobster pliers to crack open the lobster.

■ Lobsters must be cooked live or right after being killed; however, you can buy precooked lobsters. Store live lobsters in seawater (fresh water will kill them) or wrap them in a wet cloth, and keep in the refrigerator for only a few hours on a bed of ice.

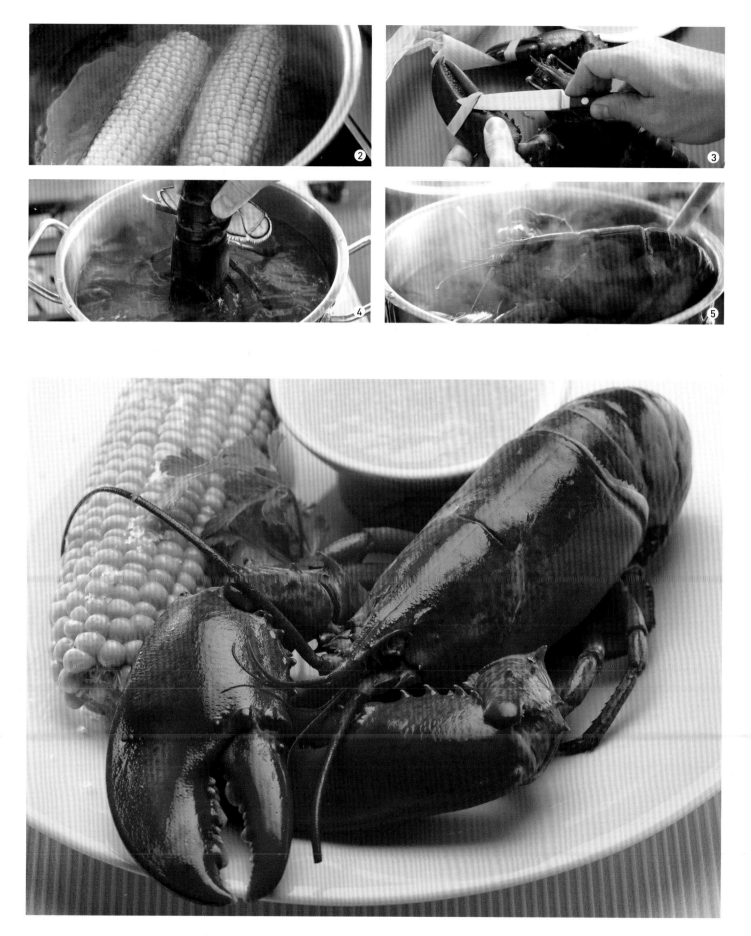

3 shallots

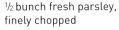 1½ celery stalks

1 leek

1 garlic clove

2 tablespoons butter

2 bay leaves

1 fresh thyme sprig

salt and pepper, to taste

4½ pounds fresh mussels, scrubbed and debearded

⅔ cup white wine

½ bunch fresh parsley, finely chopped

Mussels Steamed in White Wine

1. Peel the shallots and cut into fine strips. Slice the celery and leek into fine strips. Press the garlic clove in its skin. Melt the butter in a saucepan. Add the garlic and shallots, then add the bay leaves, thyme, celery, and leek, and sauté briefly. Season with salt and pepper.

2. Discard any mussels with broken shells and any that refuse to close when tapped. Add the mussels and mix with the vegetables. Pour in the wine, cover the pan, and let simmer for 3–5 minutes, until the mussels open. Discard any mussels that remain closed. Sprinkle the parsley over the mussels.

Mix well and serve immediately.

30

■ Use an empty mussel shell to eat the cooked mussels without cutlery.

 2 tomatoes

 2 shallots

 5 fresh basil leaves

 bunch fresh parsley

 salt and pepper, to taste

 3 tablespoons red wine vinegar

 ½ cup olive oil

 4½ pounds cooked mussels

Mussels Served Cold in a Herb Marinade

1. Peel the tomatoes, cut them into quarters, and seed and dice. Dice the shallots. Chop the basil leaves and the parsley, then combine everything in a small mixing bowl.

2. Season with salt and pepper and pour the vinegar over the tomatoes and shallots. Add the oil and mix well.

3. Discard any mussels that have not opened. Remove the cooked mussels from their shells. Place the mussels in the herb marinade, cover with plastic wrap, and chill in the refrigerator for 30 minutes.

Arrange the mussels in bowls and serve with toasted white bread.

■ This dish is especially delicious made with clams. It is particularly important not to serve them directly from the refrigerator, but at room temperature.

2 garlic cloves

bunch fresh parsley

8 cuttlefish, squid, or baby octopus

salt and pepper, to taste

1 fresh rosemary sprig, plus extra sprigs to garnish

pinch of crushed red pepper

¼ cup extra virgin olive oil

1¼ cups plain yogurt

1 lemon

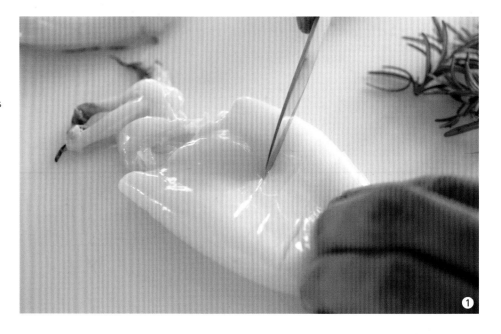

Grilled Cuttlefish

1. Peel and chop the garlic. Finely chop the parsley. Clean the cuttlefish thoroughly and dry with paper towels. Place on a work surface, smooth-side up, and make shallow slits across its width.

2. Place in a soufflé dish with the slit side on top, season with salt and pepper on the inside, fill with the parsley and half the garlic, and turn over.

3. Pluck the rosemary off the stem, combine with the crushed red pepper, and spread over the cuttlefish. Season again with salt and pepper and sprinkle 2 tablespoons of the oil over it. Marinate for 15 minutes. You can also marinate the cuttlefish the day before cooking this dish.

4. Heat a nonstick skillet, add the cuttlefish, and sear, slit-side first, then turn. Cook for about 2–3 minutes on each side.

5. Put the yogurt, the remaining garlic, and the remaining oil in a mixing bowl. Season with salt and pepper and mix.

Slice the lemon and arrange with the cuttlefish on serving plates. Garnish with rosemary sprigs and serve with the yogurt and garlic dip.

■ Cuttlefish and squid taste even more delicious when chargrilled and served with tomato vinaigrette and fresh white bread.

 2¼ pounds octopus

2 tablespoons coarse sea salt

1 lemon, halved, and 1 half sliced

1 fresh thyme sprig

1 cup white wine

1 tablespoon sweet paprika

¼ teaspoon cayenne pepper

¼ cup extra virgin olive oil

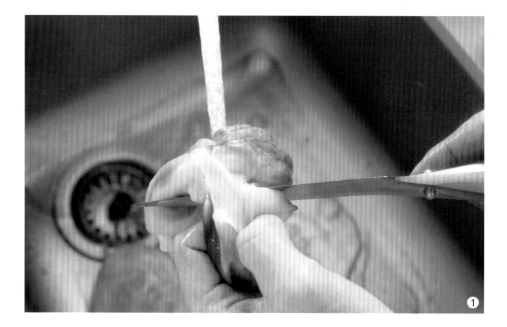

Cooked Octopus with Lukewarm Vinaigrette

1. Thoroughly wash the octopus. Turn the body inside out, pull away the entrails, and cut them off with a knife.

2. Rinse thoroughly and remove any remaining skin.

3. Pinch the lower part of the head of the octopus in order to grip the beak and remove it.

4. Bring a deep saucepan of water to a boil, then place the octopus in it with the salt, lemon slices, and thyme.

5. Simmer for about 40 minutes. Cut a piece from the octopus and taste it to check that it is cooked. To make the vinaigrette, pour the juice of half the lemon into a mixing bowl. Add the wine, paprika, and cayenne pepper. Mix with the oil and 1 tablespoon of the hot cooking liquid from the octopus. Remove the octopus from the pan, drain, and slice.

Arrange on serving plates, sprinkle with the vinaigrette, and serve immediately.

✱
✱ 70
✱

■ In Spain, cooked octopus is often served on cooked potato slices. It is also delicious when served with fresh garlic sauce or on a mixed bean salad. The cooking time depends largely on the size of the octopus. This is why it should be tasted to check that it is tender.

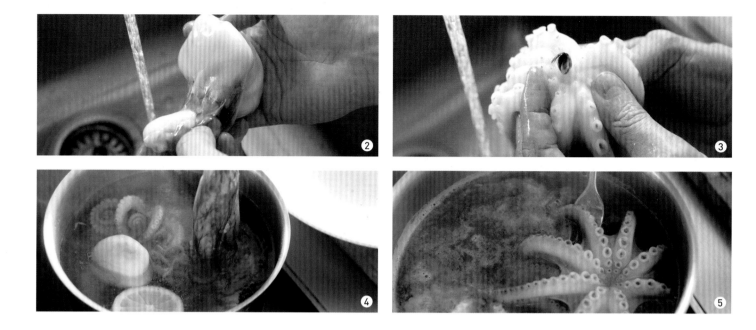

1 shallot

⅓ cup red wine vinegar

1 tablespoon water

24 oysters

Oysters on Ice

1. Peel the shallot and finely chop. Pour the vinegar into a bowl with the water, add the chopped shallot, and mix.

2. Crack the oysters with an oyster knife.

3. Open the oysters and serve on a platter with crushed ice. Place the sauce in a small bowl in the center of the platter.

■ Rock oysters such as Fines de Claires, Portugaise, Sylter Spezial, or the American Blue Point are true delicacies when eaten raw.

30

24 oysters	
2 leeks	
2 teaspoons butter	
salt and pepper, to taste	
freshly grated nutmeg	
1 cup Hollandaise sauce	
4 cups coarse sea salt (about 2¼ pounds)	

Baked Oysters

1. Open the oysters, remove from their shells, and place the oysters in a strainer. Clean the shells and place in a preheated low oven for 3–5 minutes to dry. Wash the leeks and slice diagonally into fine strips.

2. Heat the butter in a saucepan until foaming. Add the leeks, season with salt, pepper, and nutmeg, and cook until brown. Add 1¼ cups of water and simmer for 2–3 minutes, until the leeks are cooked and the liquid is reduced. Place the leeks in the oyster shells and put the oysters on top.

3. Meanwhile, preheat the broiler to medium. Pour the Hollandaise sauce over the oysters and cook for 2–3 minutes under the preheated broiler. Make sure that the oysters do not turn brown.

Spread a thick layer of sea salt over the bottom of a large platter, then put the oysters on top and serve.

■ Oysters removed from their shells can be baked like fried fish in a beer batter and served with tartar sauce, or fried wrapped in bacon and served on sauerkraut.

45

INDEX